meet me in my psyche

Hannah Gray

BookLeaf Publishing

India | USA | UK

Presentation by *BookLeaf Publishing*

Web: www.bookleafpub.com

E-mail: info@bookleafpub.com

ISBN: 9789360945633

First edition 2024

*This book goes out to all the lost souls
searching for their place in the vast
universe, and all the souls that have passed
on their way to do so.*

*In loving memory of William Aaron Gray —
August 13, 1979 - December 2, 2012.*

ACKNOWLEDGEMENT

I wouldn't be here today without all the encouragement from my therapists, family, and friends. Thank you for always guiding me even when I did not believe in myself.

I would also like to give a special thank you to my little Holden Lane, for always reminding me time and time again, how the simple things in life are the most magical of all.

PREFACE

The contents of this book contain my heart, soul, guts, and tears. The most vulnerable side of myself.

For those who understand the depths of mental health and the tragedy it can impose, for those who can feel that pain, never stop fighting. If anything is taken away after reading, I hope it's inspiration. Inspiration to reach for your dreams; finding the beauty in the darkness.

The war inside the mind is the most malicious war of all. It's you against yourself. You never know who among us is fighting a battle within themselves. Therefore, be kind and show compassion, you could be the one who changes it all.

Van Gogh

Allowing my mind to roam,
off into the meadows of the unknown;

What will I find?

Who really knows,
but I'm off on an adventure—
a journey through my psyche.

Many places are dark,
tears shower down like rainfall,
black and blue,
saturated with gloom.

Others burst with sunshine,
or glow from the moonlight,

clear skies and stars shining bright,
one of a kind painting,
showcased within my mind.

Together they meet,
creating such beautiful chaos,
much like Starry Night—
Vincent Van Gogh.

– h.b.gray

My Friend; Darkness

We meet again on the path of self destruction,
somber skies reveal *Darkness* drawing closer.

Vulnerably consciousness under gray clouds,
paralyzed by the rain that showers down.

Accepting defeat in this pitched battle,
neglecting optimism for a familiar road traveled.

Darkness and I, we're rather old friends,
hiding in the shadows from the moment life
began.

Infallibly by my side, embraced with open arms,
coexisting with *Darkness* conveys warmth.

Secure in the chaos that burdens my psyche,
a prisoner of war seduced by melancholy.

– h.b.gray

Back To My Roots

5

I think I found my way, I say,
as the shadows creep behind me.

Before I know it,
back to my roots—*lost in the darkness*.

— h.b.gray

BPD

"I'm not an evil person," I whisper after the split.
I have always been misunderstood,
crying out for help.

No one there to guide me,
every man for himself.
I truly love so deeply, my entire heart and being.

Caring, thoughtful, and nurturing,
everything I've ever sought for.
Value others more than myself—
intensely understanding.

Hypervigilant, wearing a mask,
personality mirroring.
Much like a chameleon,

I blend with my surroundings.

Peacemaker, caretaker, even the devils advocate.

Finding beauty in the pain;
until darkness engulfs my body.

Tearing me apart, piece by piece,
black is all I can perceive.
Rage, hate, resentment. I hate you. I hate me.

Who am I? An answer I'll never apprehend.

Searching for the will to live,
feeling everything in the void.

Self destructive habits,
numb the pain, numb my brain.
Aware of what I'm doing,
but too far gone to evade.

Watching as I slip, yet no energy to defy.
Furthermore—*darkness has always felt like
home.*

The only place I've ever felt like I'm not alone.

So once again, I slip into the comfort of the
shadows.

Cradled with melancholy, tightly in its arms,
a slave to the somber it brings upon.

Those not kissed by this merciless demon,
cannot fathom to understand.
They say, "suck it up, life isn't that bad."

But, all I see is black.

There is no light where I am, the only way out is
death.

Demons live inside your brain,
they tell you horrible things;
kill yourself, you're unlovable,
unworthy to breathe earth's air.

If you try to tell me differently, they will not
allow me to hear.

Instead, I'll make you believe every word,
repeated in my head.

As I wake in the morning, demons by my side,
unable to apologize,
torture holding me tight.

If you only understood this disease of the brain,

you would see I am only a child—

a child who has never been saved.

– h.b.gray

Sirens Symphony

Ankle deep, in the sea of depression.

Why did I step into the water?

I remain calm; there is no panic as the current pulls me further.

Knee deep, I hear the sound of a familiar tune.

Swim back to shore, resist the tides, or flow with the current to your demise.

Waist deep, the sound becomes more clear.

Sirens sing my name, a name they know too well.

They lure me into the sea, irresistibly comforting.

Neck deep, I sing a symphony with these sirens.

Pulled to shore on the flowery island, home at last,

in the sea of depression.

– h.b.gray

Scary Love

Trauma showcased in my reflection,
like an art exhibition,
sculpted beautifully by the cold hands of passion.

Melancholic symphony played by my heart strings,
a melody so slow and sweet.

The heart wants what the heart wants,
while the mind is the opposing force.

Another war begins within,
this war never ends.

Aching for tranquility
between my mind, body, and spirit,
yet—I'm on the front line, in a combat zone,
fighting a war I did not ask for.

My life and sanity stand on this line,
I see no white flag or peace treaties.

The heart wants what the heart wants,
sweet symphony of love.

Though the mind will not allow passage,
not without a war.

– h.b.gray

Haunting Memories

I remember how
you used to strangle me
until I couldn't breathe
unconscious

I remember how you would say
the most gut-wrenching things
in the midst of it all
eyes as black as your soul

I remember how
I walked on eggshells for years

yet still pulled out of the shower
thrown on the floor
shampoo poured in my eyes

I remember how
I would fight back
until I could fight no more

I remember the night
I shouldn't have survived
after you left the mark of the beast
scarred for life

I remember how I always loved you
tried to make it work
the little girl in me
doing as she's been taught

—h.b.gray

Out Of Air

alone I float
a soul lost in the vast universe
a room full of people
yet empty
not present in the moment
instead my mind is in space
oxygen is getting low
no memory of yesterday
last week, month, year,
my whole life
dazed and confused
nothing feels real
I don't feel real
no sense of reality
no sense of myself
no sense at all
like living in a constant dream
like being so numb that
I question if I'm even alive
I feel nothing
forgetting how to cry
completely unfazed
how do you explain something so unearthly
nobody understands
nobody knows the real me

I don't know the real me
isolated in the cage of my mind
me myself and I
and I'm running out of air
    I'm ....

        running ....

            out..

                of..

                    ...

— h.b.gray

Fumes

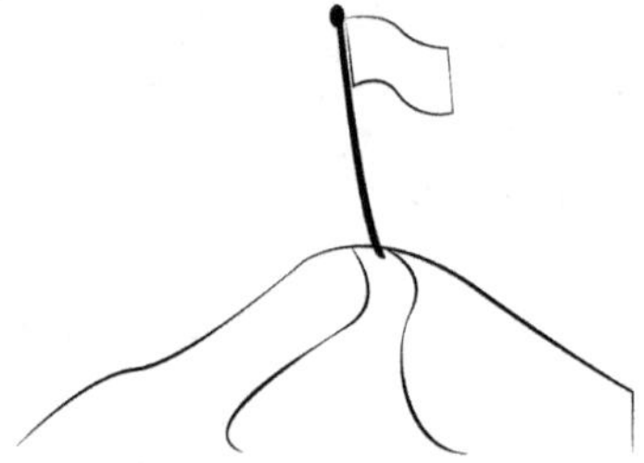

Is my mind fueling my body,
fumes to stay alive?

A stadium is created,
using the circumference of my skull,
hosting the event is my mind.

Body is weak,
eyes are heavy,
they fall shut right on time.

The event has begun,
front row seats,
observing the race around my psyche.

Lap after lap,
neck to neck,
light vs darkness,
race to the death.

Dwindling fumes,
cause tires to screech,
fragmented pieces,
indicate defeat.

Haunting words echo throughout,
piercing my ears with a shrieking sound.
"I won this race, I always will,
haven't you learned your lesson, my dear?"

Checkered flag sways to signal the end,
fire ignited from within,
shadows appear out of darkness,
self-proclaimed eternal damnation.

Much like a phoenix,
I shall burn,
before rising from the ashes.

For I now understand,
the race against darkness,
is only a race against myself.

I am the light,
I am the shadows,
I am everything in between.

The power to defeat dark forces,

begins with believing,
in *me*.

– h.b.gray

I'll Be Here

tomorrow will come,
the sun shall rise,
just as the night sky will shine,
lit up by the moonlight—

and I will still be here.

— h.b.gray

Cardinal Bird

Complete tranquility,
as I watch a cardinal,
wander around the yard.

Endlessly washing the same dish,
gazing through the window,
I catch myself whisper,
"Is it you after all?"

Just when I thought I lost sight,
you show yourself once more,
peeking out behind the trees.

Please don't leave me.

All at once,
off you go,
flying after another.

Leaving—*just as my father.*

– h.b.gray

reminder: look at the cows

twenty-five years on this earth,
going on twenty-six,
mountain of mistakes,
all burdened deep within.

every year i hope will be better than the last,
yet, somehow, someway,
an endless cycle of the past.

stress piles higher than the eye can see,
losing sight of the simple pleasures,
sunshine, laughter, and bees.

oh to be present,
present in the moment,
little feet stomping,
"look at the cow mama!"

so easy to forget how wonderful this life is,
when your trapped inside your mind,
fighting to survive,
no will to live.

–h.b.gray

Mirror Mirror On The Wall

Room full of mirrors,
my reflection,
in every direction,
yet—I do not recognize myself.

Dark like outer space,
oh, I see a twinkle,
out in the Milky Way.

How the stars shine bright, clear skies, full moon
gazing.

Dark though extraordinary.

Through the window comes light,
reflecting beauty on those hidden shadows,
like a field of wildflowers
dancing under a rainbow,
as the sun rises after a storm.

A room full of mirrors,
reflecting different parts of me,
whether it be dark or light,
beauty can be perceived.

A room full of mirrors—

I sit in peace,
embracing every single part of me.

—h.b.gray

you left me

just like the wind
blows freely
you too
floated out of my arms
to flow with the wind
yet here I stand
feet on the ground
stuck
just as you left me

and as I rest
there you are
invading my dreams
as I smile with glee
our eyes meet
a warm embrace
we dance the night away
until I wake
that's when you leave

—h.b.gray

Group Therapy

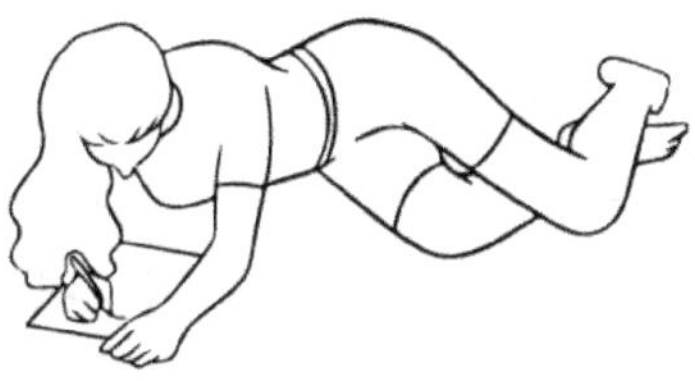

A room full of people,
I sit alone, they decompress from the weekend—
I write.

Grueling act to focus on what they say,
when in my mind,
there is no silence,
overflowing thoughts run rampant.

Feeling as if today I cannot speak,
nevertheless, I can write.

Mumbled voices in the distance,
chills cover my body,
searching for warmth within –
pencil to paper; start the fire.

Healing the trauma,
one word at a time,
as I pour my heart onto paper,
and sit in silence with my thoughts.

–h.b.gray

Silver Linings

No one talks about the grief you feel when you
are finally happy.

When it feels like things are headed towards the
light.

When you see the light; touch the light.

No one talks about the grief—

The grief,
that comes when you walk away from situations,
no longer aligned with your path.

Finally choosing you. It almost feels wrong.

But yet—nothing has ever felt more right.

There is a somber cloud floating over you, a
silver lining shining through.

You say goodbye to the darkness; hello to the
light.

No one talks about the grief—

I think we should.

– h.b.gray

when you know you know

a phrase i never quite understood,
until i met you.
such an obscure moment,
yet you felt so familiar.
complete strangers,
souls intertwined,
lovers in a past life.
for i seen you,
in all of me.
guided by the universe,
stars aligned,
to meet once again,
symbolically in present time.
faintest idea what the future holds,
however,
i see you at the end of my road.
walk with me,

frail and feeble.
hold my hand,
through armageddon.
we shall not say goodbye,
merely see you soon.
i'll be in nirvana,
awaiting you.

– h.b. gray

i wonder

sometimes i wonder if i've always been this way

if i was only born to feel pain
and to give love to others
only to be neglected in return

sometimes i wonder if i'm even alive
or simply trapped in an endless hell loop

i wonder if my soul died long ago
if i'm only a walking corpse
of what could have been

sometimes i wonder
why things have to be this way

–h.b.gray

Ode to Perks Of Being A Wallflower

I daydream about how life would be if I was
normal.

If I was raised in a normal household,
with normal parents,
the "normal" life.

I pretend to be normal,
some would say I carry myself well.
Too well.

So well you'd never know,
all the horrors I have lived through,
the hands of darkness I've fallen victim to.

I'm so resilient they say,
though I crumble to pieces after the charades.

What a curse,
what a blessing,
to think and feel so deeply.

To be able to experience the depths of pain,
as you seep further into the darkness within.

Feeling every feeling that comes out to play,
becoming addicted to the melancholy,
that haunts you all day.

*You could say there is perks to being the
wallflower—*

if only you find the beauty in the darkness.

(don't let it consume you)

—h.b.gray

sticks and stones

i wish you could understand how deeply I feel,
how deeply things affect me,
sticks and stones may break my bones
just as feeling can shatter my soul.

–h.b.gray

Mother Nature's Dance

I danced in the rain for so long,
I forgot how to dance in the sun.

I must learn to dance,
with the grass and the trees,
as the sun shines down before me.

Barefoot in a flowery field,
pick a dandelion,
make a wish.

Twirl around,
feel the sun kiss your skin,
embrace mother nature,
for we are one.

Be as free as the wind,
bright as the moon,
flow like the rivers,
bloom from your roots.

—h.b.gray

Sing the Blues

I sing the blues, at night,
while thinking of you.

I sing the blues, in the morning,
as I open my eyes,
you on my mind.

I sing the blues so much—I am blue.

Thinking about you,

while you're thinking about *her.*

— h.b.gray

Writing Heals

I feel the pain,
I write it down,
it flows effortlessly,
I don't scream nor shout.

I feel the love,
I write it down,
the paper knows,
I'm vulnerable deep down.

I feel everything,
I write to heal.

Pouring my guts out onto paper,
where it feels safe to spill.

— h.b.gray

"i don't understand you"

be glad you don't understand the extent of my
psyche;

it would drive one mad who is not used to
darkness.

— h.b.gray

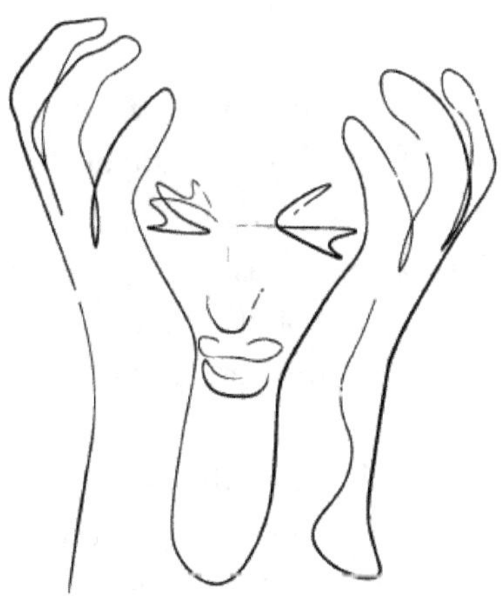

skeptic thinking

water glistening
silver lining gleaming
as the sky turns orange
the day turns to night

sailboats as far as the eye can see
out on this lake
a warm spring day

i look to the sky
as the sun beams through the clouds
i look to the water
boats sailing near and far

thinking to myself

there is no way there isn't a god

sincerely—
a skeptic searching for something to believe in.

— h.b.gray

Banana Pudding

When was the last time I felt alive?

I truly cannot tell.

Have I ever felt alive?

Or only surviving in Hell?

I whisk together pudding,
slice bananas,
lay wafers in the pan.

Window cracked,
I feel the cool spring breeze,
sweet and dandy.

A breath of fresh air—
breath of life.
Maybe I am alive,
only too trapped in mind,
to experience living.

Maybe this isn't a living hell,
only my perception.

Because the wind blows freely,
just as I,
energy intertwined,
I feel alive.

Who knew banana pudding
could bring such an epiphany.

Who knew fresh air on a sunny day
could make you feel alive.

— h.b.gray

who am i

do you ever wish upon a star
someone somewhere could come down
to tell you who you are
everyday i wonder
who am i
who am i supposed to be
who do i want to be
people tell me all the time
they love who i am
i'm such a good person
they love the person they know as me
but i am not that person
when i am alone i don't recognize myself
the reflection i see is that of a stranger
closet full of masks
one for each group of people
hanging them up when i come home

leaving me bare and raw and confused
a stranger to myself
occasionally i embody the mask
try to become that version
however i always end up bare again
i've been so many different people
i just want to be me
but the question persists
who am i

— h.b.gray

Holden Lane

Born in November,
my scorpio baby,
a precious boy—
changing my life forever.

I always hoped,
hoped he would be nothing like me.
The wild child,
with anger like no other.

Though a blessing in disguise,
I have come to learn.
For I can love him,
as I wished to be loved.

Parenting him;
reparenting myself,
together we grow—
together we thrive.

My sweet little boy,
big brown eyes,
mama loves you,
to infinity and beyond.

— h.b.gray

beautifully you

beauty is in everything
happiness found in the smallest moments
staring in the mirror finally seeing
you
glowing skin
eyes full of life
beautifully you

— h.b.gray

Samantha's Poem

i look in the mirror
only to see
a standing shell
of who i used to be

exposing my body
an uncomfortable task
when the clothing is removed
i see the past

once unblemished skin
now is defected
displaying a hole
i wasn't protected

fighting this battle

inside my mind
heart aching more
as the days go by

he says he loves me
yet his actions conflict
genuine love
doesn't leave a hole in your chest.

— h.b.gray

Regeneration

do you ever think about your mortal expiration
date?
you know, the day you finally get to heaven's
gates,
or hell fire,
nirvana,
or nothing at all.

the day everything goes black.
nothing to see, nothing to hear,
all sensations seize to exist.
your mortality expires.

why do i wish for the angel of death to appear so
often?

the strongest houses eventually crumble,
a storm comes through,
blows off the roof,
everything collapses.

let's say the house is well-maintained,
roofs can be repaired.
in most cases, however,
the house is poorly upkept.

stood tall through many storms,
cracks in the foundation.
walls bend and break,
stress weighs down profoundly.

the strongest house is now scattered about.
how do you begin to restore such demolition?
there are no blueprints or instructions,
can it be refurbished?

helping hands feel too far away to deal with such
a burden.

some witnessed the roof torn off,
walls bending,
foundation cracking.
yet, perplexed when the house pummels down to
dirt.

earth however,
absorbs the pieces,
planting them in the soil.

sprouting roots,
regeneration transpires of the house there before.

slow and steady,
on a journey to stand high,
progressing forward,
mending broken pieces left behind.

good as new,
minor blemishes,
illustrate the beauty in tragedy.

full of character,
the house is now stronger than ever.

crumble and fall,
soak in the soil,
learn from misfortunes of rock bottom.

the little boy that calls me mama,
needs a home to evolve in.

sprout your roots,
trust the universe,

regeneration will happen.

day by day,
minute by minute,
growth progresses.

storms come through from time to time,
reinforcements are intact.
thus today is not the day,
mortality reaches the final chapter.

— h.b.gray

in this moment, i am grounded

imagine that you are a plant,
tree, shrub, flower,
whatever plant you desire to be,
you are that plant.

your feet are roots,
grounded deep within the earth,
you become one with nature,
peacefully and gracefully growing.

the sun rises casting a warm glow upon you,
wind gently blows through your petals or leaves,
bees and butterflies settle onto you,
such small majestic beings.

you stay grounded,
in awe of the beauty found within nature,
in awe that the sunshine, grassy plains,
mountains, and bodies of water,
are the most magical of all.

you are present in the moment,
accepting that, you are, in fact,
a force of nature,

filled with beauty and uniqueness,
character found in each thorn, leaf, petal, or
branch.

storms pass through here and there, however;
your roots are planted deeply into earth's crust,
thunder and lightning strike and rumble,
just as the sun shall rise once more.

i ask of you, to imagine yourself as a plant,
to stay grounded, present, and most of all,
embrace the fact that—you are a force of nature,
even on the darkest, coldest, nights.

i, myself, will do the same.

i will grow in the sunshine,
keep grounded during storms,
be present in the moment,
as each day passes on.

— h.b.gray

I miss you

I miss you in the mornings,
as I open my eyes.
I miss you in the evenings,
when I turn off the lights.

I miss you when the grief,
creeps onto my back,
leaving me thinking of us,
and the time that has passed.

Your memory haunts me,
you never go away,
like crashing tides in my mind,
should I have stayed?

Our lives are so different,
yet the same in a way.

I am by myself,
while you're out to play.

This life is lonely,
without you by my side,
but then I remember—

I was lonely the whole time.

— h.b.gray

You Can't Rush Grief

You can't rush grief, though you can try.
Numb it, use distractions,
or face it head on.

Despite it all,
you can't rush grief,
No—it'll get you on a sunny day
when you're glowing with joy.

On the beach,
full of zen,
oh wait, you're never coming back.

That song that comes on,
while driving the backroads,
i'm reminded of you again.

years pass, time flies by,
yet stands still all at once.

it's 2024 but in my head,
i'm fourteen and it's 2012.

— h.b.gray

Home

i said you felt like home
as if it were a compliment

i said you felt like home
but not the home you're thinking of

i said you felt like home
as you opened the door
to the chaos living inside of me

hidden away amongst the shadows
kept a bay behind the walls
there is a little girl screaming
help me i feel so alone

i said you felt like home
then you slammed the door
in the little girl's face

alone she stands,
only her and the shadows,
yearning for compassion—
home sweet home.

— h.b.gray

flashbacks of you

i hate how i don't remember anything
until it hits me at midnight
just as i close my eyes
a deer in the headlights

i hate how i remember everything
my body remembers as well
fight or flight full survival mode
but i'm laying in bed safe and sound

i hate how i'm brought back to the moment
but i have to feel it to heal

i hate how you started a war
and now i'm responsible for
rebuilding what you destroyed

— h.b.gray

Sunday Scaries

Sunday afternoon;
I feel nothing, I feel everything, I am numb.

Desiring to help myself,
desiring to self-destruct,
seeking the balance—Libra in my blood.

Indecisiveness eats me alive,
as I rot in this bed thinking about life.

The sun is shining, flowers have bloomed,
but I'm stuck in December—filled with gloom.

Sunday afternoon; trying to stay positive,
the shadows are talking, I lend a listening ear.

Sunday afternoon; I don't want to feel,
I don't want to slip into the shadows,
back home with my friends.

Quite and peaceful just as I wished,
yet everything in me screams,
"let chaos win!"

Healing is hard, suffering is harder,

sometimes they intertwine,
you must trust the process.

Chaos will not win the battle today,
For I am at peace, at peace I will stay.

— h.b.gray

Sunshine Psyche

one day it's dark,
actually, it's been dark, for months,
so dark that one could not see in front of them.

however now—
now, there is light.

at the flip of a switch what was once dark—is
bright.

the gloomy cloud has passed,
the rain has stopped,
beautiful rainbows begin to appear.

sunlight glistens over the waterfront,
the sunlight that makes brown eyes turn to
honey,
warmth of light that gives you hope,

fills you full of glee.

the shadows hide away,
the light is beaming,
i can see again,
i can slow down.

i can feel positivity in all that surrounds me.

beauty is in this life,
beauty is all around.

skies turn to cotton candy,
lovers turn to home.

no longer lost,
everything i have longed for,
lays before me.

i see clearly again.

this is who i am.

i am the sunshine,
the light,
the gleeful warmth.

the switch flipped,
my light is now on,

newfound happiness shines from within,
a greater hope for tomorrow.

— h.b.gray

The Day My World Stopped Spinning

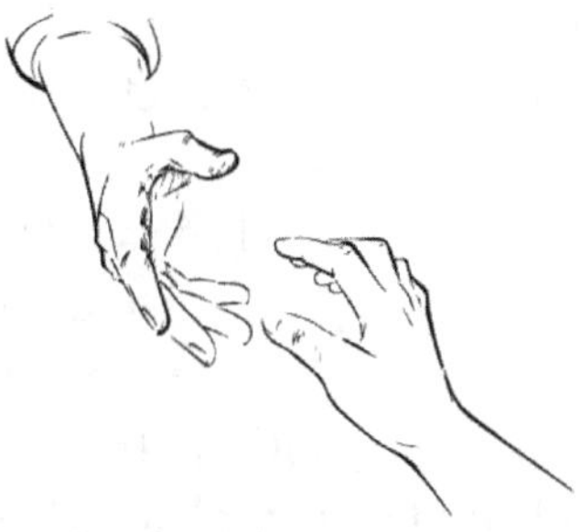

December 2, 2012. I remember this day all too
well, and December 3, 2012, which is strange
because I don't remember most of my life. These
two days however, are clear, vivid, like watching
a movie in IMAX. A movie that haunts me to
this very day.

Let's start with December 2. Abby and I were at
Granny's. It was a Sunday afternoon, the phone
rang. It was you. Mama was just arriving at
Granny's to pick us up and take us back home
with her. I remember Granny asking if I wanted
to talk to you, I did not. I was handed the phone,
but I had nothing to say to you. I was hurt,
angry, and sad. I told you I was mad at you. Mad
because you left once again to go raise a child

who wasn't even your own. You left me. You left us. You said you'd be coming home for Christmas, I was happy about that, excited even. I have always been a Daddy's girl, all I wanted was my Daddy home. Since I didn't want to talk to you, you asked to talk to Mama. I walked the phone out to her and let y'all talk. I remember Mama smiling and laughing while speaking with you. I later found out you had asked her to marry you again. She loved you, and truthfully now looking back, she would have married you again in a heartbeat. After y'all got off the phone, Abby and I loaded up in the car with Mama and headed home. The entire ride home I was still mad, but also very excited because in a few short weeks I'd get to see you again. So I thought anyway.

December 3, 2012. Monday morning, I was awoken with my phone being taken away. I had no idea what I had done wrong for my phone to be taken, I was very confused. Mama looked like she had been crying all night. Her eyes were swollen and red. She couldn't tell me why she took my phone from me, so being the teenager that I was, of course I was irritated. I asked her what was wrong, she said she had a toothache all night and didn't get any sleep. I got ready for school like it was a normal day. I remember I was wearing hot pink pants, a black shirt, and black boots. We left home, the same time as usual, like we were headed to school. I would have never guessed the horrors that awaited us. We stopped at Nana's, this was unusual, especially since we were going to be late for school at this point. I remember being so agitated because not only do I not have my phone, now I'm going to be late for school. After Nana's, we stopped at Granny's. Immediately I knew something was wrong. Aunt Sam's car was in the driveway, she lived in Kentucky at this time so why was she there? Granny was sitting on the porch in her pajamas, housecoat, and slippers. We got out of the car, and Granny's face looked just like Mama's. Eyes red and swollen like she'd been crying all night. Now I am aware this is not another toothache. It was never a toothache.

Granny tells us to go in and sit on her bed. Abby and I do as were told, we sit on the end of her bed. Granny then proceeds to kneel down in front of us, touching the both of us with her hands, and says, "Your Daddy was in an accident, and he didn't make it." I finally understand why my phone was taken, why everyone's eyes were red and swollen, why everything that morning was a bit off. My world just went black. My heart shattered. Everything inside me died that day. That is the first time I ever had thoughts of suicide. Fourteen years old, and my Daddy had died. I didn't even get to tell him goodbye. He died thinking that I hated him. I did not get to tell him I loved him, I missed him, I just wanted him to come home. I refused to speak to him when I had the chance just hours before he departed from this world. He died not knowing how much he meant to me. After we were told of the tragedy that occurred, we had to go home and pack our bags. We were going to Illinois. The bags were packed and we headed back to Granny's, but now Papa was home too. A sound that I will never forget, is the sound of a grown man I have never seen shed one single tear, screaming, sobbing, and wailing. The sound of him mourning his son was loud enough to hear from outside of the house. To this day I can still hear his cries.

The week following your death is a blur. I remember key moments. I remember Aunt Sam nearly killing us trying to drive to the court house. You were actually going to court to see if the child you left Tennessee for was yours. I remember staying at Silly Willy's and everyone went to view your body, but we were not allowed to go. I remember them talking about your body being "mangled." I remember sitting at Silly Willy's kitchen table trying to help pick songs to play at your funeral. I remember going to pick out your casket. I remember picking out your favorite cologne to spray on you. I remember when we had your visitation in Illinois and we were the first to view you. I remember not being able to walk down the aisle, nearly falling to my knees, sobbing my eyes out. That could not be MY Daddy laying in this casket. No. Not mine. But it was. Thankfully, Aunt Sam was there to pick me up and help me walk. She still does that to this day. I remember finally leaving, and Mama was the last person to say goodbye to you. We all gave her privacy. I remember going out to eat with everyone afterward and we all took a picture with the signature Billy Gray middle finger.

We brought you back home to Tennessee, in the bed of Papa's truck. I remember riding behind it and still not believing that you were in that casket, you were really gone. I remember burying you, six feet in the ground. You were home for Christmas that year, just not the way I had expected. I remember everything, and sometimes, I wish I didn't.

Since you've been gone, it does feel like the world has stopped spinning. I died that day and I don't think I have ever come back to life yet. In fact, everyone died. A piece of every single one of us died on December 2, 2012. Some have handled your death better than others, but nonetheless, not one of us is okay. You do not expect to bury your father as a teenager. A parent does not expect to bury their child. Siblings do not expect to bury their brother at such a young age. Especially, when you're completely blindsided by it.

I always sit and wonder about the "what if's." What if you were still alive? Would things be as bad as they are? Would I be the way that I am? Would our family be as dysfunctional as it is now? The "what if's" and "why's" will eat you alive if you're not careful. I have had my fair share of being eaten alive by them. I have had to accept that I cannot change what has happened, I cannot go back in time. I just have to believe you're still here with me, believe that you know I love you and I always have, believe that you are in a better place.

You turned the last page of your book here on earth. I will cherish that book forever, hold it tightly in my soul. This December will mark 12 years, and I miss you more than I could ever put into words. I am still my Daddy's little girl. I always will be. You were the first man I loved, and the first to break my heart. Unfortunately, grief never goes away, time does not fade the emotions and feelings. However, it is how you deal with the grief that is the key. Truth be told, I have not handled it very well. I have cursed God's name, lost faith in everything, spiraled into destructive habits. Lots of times just HOPING it would in some sense bring me closer to you. I am now hoping one day my world will begin to spin again, maybe life will form in the parts of me that died. I will keep trying down here on earth, remember your legacy, for I am just as hard headed and stubborn as you. In the meantime, it is what it is. I will take it day by day until we meet again. When that day comes, be prepared for a fight, because you left me here without you. But also, tears, laughter, and most of all an abundance of love. For I will never let you go.

Your little girl,
Hannah Gray

10
Unidades .

O GRANDE RESET!

CONTROLE DA MENTE - DOMONIO MUNDIAL - ESTERILIZACAO EXPOSTA!